Nikki,
Thank you for being such a [   ] my
life! I love you so muc[   ]

615-738-6131 ♡ Much love,
Brooke

P.S. Thank you for
all the laughs, talks, +
encouragement....
And don't forget
about us playing
Cards! Fun times! ☺

Lonely

Traveler

By

Brooksie D. Thompson

"The pain that you've been feeling can't compare to
the joy that's coming" - Romans 8:18

"When you go through deep waters, I will be
with you" - Isaiah 43:2

Keep the faith

♡ Much love,
Brooksie D. Thompson

COVER, AUTHOR, & RAILROAD TRACK PHOTOGRAPH CREDITS
Rick's Photography

PHOTOGRAPH LOCATION
Downtown Lawrenceburg, TN
And
David Crockett State Park
Lawrenceburg, TN

FOREWORD
Dr. Martin Cortez Wesley

AUTHOR BIO & BOOK BLURB
Jesi Jayy

LONELY TRAVELER
Copyright © 2017 by Brooksie D. Thompson
Original publish date
November 1, 2017

OTHER BOOKS BY BROOKSIE D. THOMPSON

The Unknown She: Shares Her Soul

and

She Speaks: To the World

Lonely Traveler is dedicated in loving memory
of my dad, Billy W. Thompson "Wild Bill"

ACKNOWLEDGEMENTS

I would like to take a moment to thank everyone who has been involved in the Lonely Traveler's book process: my family and friends who support me; those in my professional circle; the School of Counseling at University of the Cumberlands; and everyone who reads and shares my books. None of this would be possible without you.

To each of you, I extend a personal thank you.

FOREWORD

Loneliness and suffering is a part of the human condition. It is part of what makes us human, but can also be the door to finding peace and happiness. It is our ability to often explore the depths of despair and grief, before we can appreciate wellness. Poetry transcends the words on the paper and helps create affective pictures on the mind which take us to dark places and images of hope.

Ms. Thompson, a professionally trained counselor and poet, has a gift for painting clear pictures of mental health darkness while also helping people to learn from these experiences and appreciate life even more. In her latest book, Lonely Traveler, she takes her reader down her own journey of depression, grief and loneliness to educate and inform those with similar experiences. Those dark experiences which make us human and bring us to a greater appreciation of life, love, family, and friends. In one poem, entitled "Time", she also shares with us how time is the greatest gift we, as humans, can give to others. We all have only a few days to live on this earth, and it is our precious time that gives life.

Martin Cortez Wesley Ph.D., LPCC-S, LCADC, NCC, MAC, DCC

Dean of the School of Counseling

University of the Cumberlands

Williamsburg, Kentucky

TABLE OF CONTENTS

"It's back"

Despite the good times and the fun she's had

It's apparent the depression is back

No one sees her at night

But it's still the tears she fights

Her emotions need to be felt

And her body needs to be held

Her pain unfolds in the most unkind ways

And steals the joy of each new day

Depression is the robber of joy and peace

It doesn't care what you need

It takes and it takes until there is nothing left but a shell

A shell of a person in a living hell

Day in and day out, she falls deeper

Into the depression, it's a trap that keeps her

It keeps her from enjoying life

And causes her and everyone she knows strife

Torturous, unrelenting sadness overtakes her

Through her broken heart, hidden tears and quieted screams, she begs for someone to save her

5-1-16

"TIME"

The greatest gift you could ever give me is your limited time

Here, I'll share some of mine

Every day that we live is closer to the day we die

Thank you for sharing so much of your time

There's no one else I'd rather share it with than you

I wonder, is that the greatest gift you can receive too?

Have you ever thought about it in that way?

Or is it just another passing day?

Spend time with those you love

Create memories to carry with you up above

5-13-16

"GYPSY SOUL"

She has a gypsy soul
And a heart of gold
She wanders from one place to the next
Never knowing where she will find rest
When you're scared
She'll be there
Think her up in your head
What would she have said?
She'd say everyone has those days
You'll be ok
And when night falls
Into the bed you'll crawl
She'll hold you in your dreams
You will quiet your screams
Because you are her
Only you can create inner peace

5-16-16

"WHEN GRIEF COMES"

When grief comes in waves
It's like a slap in the face that takes your breath away
It's your back to the door
As you make your way to the floor
It doesn't care who you are
It will always break your heart
It's makes you cry and scream
It makes it hard to breathe
You call a friend to help you get through
She prays over you
She tells you to breathe
In your nose and out your mouth, it doesn't come with ease
Something so simple as breathing in and out is made so hard
Like I said, grief doesn't care who you are
It takes your mind back to that place
Your guard was down, you weren't safe
My grief is worse at night
But I find comfort in knowing I'm not alone in the fight

5-28-16

"PRAY"

When you wake in the middle of the night

With a lot on your mind

There's no better way

To spend your time than to pray

Pray for family, friends, and strangers

Pray the Lord keep them safe from danger

You know they've been struggling lately

Pray for clarity and safety

Pray for peace of mind

Tell them you prayed for them and they'll be fine

Let them know you're not waiting anymore

You're praying, right now

Right now, in the middle of the night

They're on your mind

5-30-16

"RELIVING THAT DAY"

Fighting back tears with all that I can
Feels like I'm reliving that day all over again
It's been eight years without you
When you left, a part of me died too
You were the best friend a girl could have
I'd give anything to have you back
Now, I watch your kids grow up through pictures
It's not the same without you near
They say time heals
That sure isn't how I feel
It feels the same as it did back then
The last time I saw you was way back when
When I graduated high school
I thought I was so cool
We laughed until we cried
You held me up in the air and I said "I can fly"
That was the last time
That night we were so alive
Now you're gone
And I can't seem to move on
I can't get past the way that you left
I never handle this day well, the day of your death
Your body's been laid to rest
I can't wait to see you again and hug your neck
Tonight, I fight
I'm continuing to fight the tears that woke me last night

5-31-16

"I'M A TREE IN A ROCK"

I'm a tree in a rock

Don't laugh, don't mock

I had the courage to stand alone

I managed to make it and grow on my own

Despite the odds,

I'm standing tall

I'll continue to be the best tree I can be

Despite the hand dealt to me

7-12-16

"TIRED"

When I told you I was tired and you asked why

You didn't know it, but I started to cry

You asked if I was tired of living

You didn't know the answer, but I can't keep on giving

Giving more and more of myself

Sometimes I just feel like I need a little help

Especially now, the devil is fighting hard for me

Doesn't he know my Father is Heavenly?

I guess that's why he fights harder everyday

I don't want to lose my way

Not again

It feels like the spirits are tearing me open, not letting me mend

What you see most of the time is a smile

But inside, that's not how I'm feeling, it hasn't in a while

Let me get to tomorrow

Maybe my heart won't feel as sorrowed

Keep me in your prayers and on your mind

Pray that tomorrow I'll be fine

8-17-16

"DEPRESSION LESSONS"

All alone in this place

Sitting in darkness with a tear stained face

Tired and torn

My mind, body and spirit are worn

Worn by daily struggles

That just cause more trouble

Stupid depression

Haven't you taught me enough lessons?

Rid yourself of me

Go away and let me be!

For years, you and I have fought and have been intertwined

The scars you have given me have taught me I'll be fine

Those scars don't define who I am or what I can do

As much as I hate you,

I guess I wouldn't have known that without you

I am strong, capable, compassionate and giving

Depression, why don't you want me living?

You're the devil fighting for a child of the King

It is for Him my heart will continue to sing

What have you done for me?

Nothing that can take me away from the King

8-17-16

"LOVING YOU"

Loving you through my fears

Loving you through my tears

No matter what, I'll keep loving you

And no matter what, I know you love me too

Thank you for allowing the time I need

Thank you for taking the lead

Thank you for loving all of me

Even the scars you cannot see

Thank you for taking the time

To pray for me at night

Thank you for being a part of my life

Thank you for lessening my strife

To have you in my life is a pleasure

God surely has blessed me beyond measure

God knew what He was doing when He put us together

Best friends and family forever

8-18-16

"BEAUTIFUL RELEASE"

As far as one can see

The sea,

The sky

So vast, so high

Beauty abundantly surrounds,

Rocks on the ground,

Birds flying,

Waves crashing,

The sound of nature and peace

Take over me

It's a beautiful release

There for the world to see

Go there and see where it takes your mind

Inside there is more beauty to find

9-3-16

"IT'S WAITING"

You are so beautiful, even in the darkness of the night

Your soul shines so bright

You'll know what to do when the situation arises

I know you will, it's inside hiding

It's waiting for that moment of peace and clarity

It's waiting for the light to see

To see what needs to be done

I know waiting is no fun

But you have it my dear

You'll know what to do when it's here

May your faith always guide you

In knowing what to do

Put your cares down for now my dear

They're not yours to bear

These struggles that you're going through

Are theirs, not meant for you

9-11-16

"PEACE IN CHAOS"

Let me sit here in the trees and breeze and open my mind

This journey in the peaceful garden is yours, not mine

I hope you get what you need

I pray you receive peace

Stay as long as you need

I'm in no hurry, it also brings peace to me

Peace in a different way

Peace that escapes us everyday

Is being brought to us now

Here in nature as the sun goes down

Right here in the small piece of paradise hidden from the town

Ahh, do you feel that

Grass under your feet?

Do you hear the creatures making their sounds?

Do you hear the bells ringing somewhere across town?

Do you see all of the beautiful trees

That will soon be losing their leaves?

Do you see the birds flying high

Way up in the night falling sky?

Take it all in,

Peace in chaos, my friend

9-11-16

"NIGHT AROUND ME FALLS"

As night around me falls,

Pumpkin pie and ice cream at Henpeck calls

They know me here

I love it, so full of cheer

Greeted by hugs and a warm smile

Make the evening here after work worthwhile

It's been a long day

But this makes a nice segway to the interstate

Many miles ahead for this young lady

That's ok, my family is back home waiting

Tomorrow is a new day, a fresh start

Thank God for kind hearts

Tomorrow I get to watch my brother play ball

I get to see the boys of fall

But for tonight,

After dessert I'll go see my best friend sing in the moonlight

Then head off for my two hour drive

Driving country roads

Taking me home, where I want to go

9-16-16

"SHINING IN THE LIGHT"

I see the sun peeking through the trees

I feel you in the gentle breeze

I hear the leaves

Blowing in the wind

I know that's you my dear friend

That's you trying to find a way

A way to let me know you're ok

A way to let me know you're safe

Thank you for letting me know

Maybe, now, it's time for me to let you go

Go to the other side

Go to the shining light

I love you and I'll see you again

Shining in the light my dear friend

9-25-16

"TOO SOON"

My dearest cousin, you left too soon

The only lights shining now are the sun and the moon

They shine on your stone during the day and the night

They still keep your spirit shining bright

It's been 10 years, and I'm just starting to cry

As I sit here and look you in the eyes

A soldier, brother, son, cousin, and friend

So many hearts are still trying to mend

I remember you as a boy of fall

Before you left, you were trying to teach me football

Though it's football time in Tennessee,

It's never felt the same to me

It's time for me to get back on the road

But brings me comfort knowing someone's been here and that you're not alone

I love you, cousin, you're in my heart

Keeping you there means we're never far apart

9-25-16

"FAITH"

Wherever you go, there I'll be

I'm in your heart, you see

Though you cannot see or feel

It is through faith that you heal

Faith,

It's those giant leaps you take

The leaps that take you where you want to go

The ones that tell your spirits to be bold

Be bold and don't hold back

Don't fear what you think you lack

Fear is a terrible thing

It can change your life in a blink

Continue to soar on the wings of faith

Knowing you'll get there you won't be late

You have God watching over you

You have His word that guides you in what to do

Stay with Him for life

He is the only one who can lessen your strife

He is the healer of the lands

After all, He created it in His hands

In His image we are made

Just remember to keep the faith

Keep it until you reach your judgment day

Keep it burning, don't let it fade

Don't let it fade into something you knew and forgot

Keep your faith burning hot

Keep believing in what you cannot see

Keep believing and let it be

Though your faith may be small

It stands strong, mighty and tall

Believe it with all of your might

And you'll rest easier at night

I know nights are hard for you

You get restless and don't know what to do

That's when you hit your knees and pray

Pray to God to keep you safe

Safe from your fears and guide the paths you take

Pray for peace and clarity

Pray this for everybody

We all fight battles no one else knows about

Except the Father, who helps us out

Whether that's by answered or unanswered prayers

Know He is there

He's watching over you

Rest, knowing someone else is praying for you too

He'll be where you are

He's inside your heart

9-28-16

"BACK TO HOPE"

Back to that place that you used to go

Back to that place that gave you hope

Sitting here on a concrete table

You taught me I was able

Able to follow my dreams

Thanks for never giving up on me

It feels nice sitting in the gentle cool breeze

And hearing the birds chirping

With hummingbirds, chipmunks, and squirrels making an appearance

I hope they don't feel like I'm an interference

Then you show up asking, are you early or am I late?

I was early, I just couldn't wait!

10-1-16

"Moments"

Life is but a compilation of moments
Don't do with them something you'll regret
Moments make memories that last
Make sure you leave a good name with your dash
The dash on the stone says you were here
It tells from year to year
When you were born and when you passed
Make an impression that lasts
But before you go
Make sure to give God your soul
Good deeds aren't enough to get in
Into the golden gates of Heaven
I pray I see you there in the sky
I pray we never truly have to say bye

10-1-16

"WHAT A DAY"

What a day it has been

I'm blessed with such loving friends

Friends that I haven't seen in years

Welcomed me with warm smiles and good cheer

Back to the place I called home for a couple of years

Brings back so many memories and joyful tears

Lots of laughter and smiles

Makes the trip feel like a lot less miles

It reminds me of why I called this place home

Because it was, for so long

My friends here love me for me

They love me unconditionally

It's a feeling I would have never known

If I hadn't made this my home

Thank you God for blessing me with more than I deserve

Thank you God for answering prayers only you could have heard

10-1-16

"JOY TO MY EARS"

Oh, the beauty of the piano music playing is so joyful to my ears

Thank you Lord for allowing me to hear

Thank you for allowing me to be where I am

Thank you for allowing me to be in Your house

10-2-16

"SEE YA LATER DAD"

The sun is shining

The wind is blowing

I know it's your way

Of telling me you're ok

Your weary body has been laid to rest

Now the true test comes for Britnee and me

Hopefully we can be what you wanted us to be

Daddy, I know you're with your mom now

You always wanted to be somehow

I tried my best to make your final wishes come true

I played Desperado 4 times in my ear as we followed you

Here I am now, sitting with you, on the ground

Writing and listening to nature sounds

I know you're finally at peace

That gives me solace and serenity

I love you daddy and know you love us too

I'll be looking for you in the night moon

See ya later dad

Thank you for sharing the heart you had

A heart so full of love and life

A heart that stopped beating on this side

The love will always remain

I'm thanking God for your wings

11-4-16

"GRIEF DOESN'T DISCRIMINATE"

Grief doesn't discriminate

It doesn't care if you're 1 or 98

It comes in waves

With tears streaming down your face

And a hurting heart,

You suddenly feel torn apart

Those once quieted screams

Are now a harsh reality

It's a reminder of the loss you have felt

It's a reminder of the cards you've been dealt

There's only one who can lessen the pain

Remember to call upon His name

He will be with you

Just allow him to

11-20-16

"FRIEND"

The scars are on her skin
From not letting others in
She couldn't be her own friend
They are there for a reason
Each came in a different season
The highs and lows
Took their toll
For years, she turned to self-harm
Scars cover her legs, stomach and arm
They're proof she made it through
And proof you can too
But don't go back to the addiction
Dream it out, do you see a vision?
There's a whole new life out there
Maybe someday you'll find it somewhere
In a place you least expect it,
You'll finally get your respite
Rest until then,
Try to be your own friend

12-13-16

"SMILE"

What's it like to smile?
I haven't been able to in a while
The ugly scowl on my face,
Has somehow taken its place
Will it ever come back?
Or is it something I will forever lack?
Remind me of how it feels
Remind me of how it can make hearts heal
I'm waiting to smile again
Please tell me it's just a matter of when

12-17-16

"ANOTHER YEAR"

Another year of agony

Another year of grief

Another year of upset

And being uneased

Another year of depression

Another year of fear

That's what comes for me with another year

12-19-16

"TOO TIRED"

Sliding, hiding

No longer confiding

Flying low, under the radar

Seems to me I haven't come very far

Mind becoming more blank each day

I guess it's trying to protect me in a different way

Forgotten, are things of the past

Maybe memories weren't really made to last

Living on the edge of anxiety and fear

Silences my ability to hear

Anything outside of what's in my head

Maybe things are better left unsaid

I'm too tired to talk and form words of thoughts

Too tired to keep fighting what needs to be fought

Too tired to even be

Too tired, so, existing is what you see

1-19-17

"WAVES"

Grief comes in waves

For no one will it wait

It'll hit when you least expect

Just when you thought you were beginning to forget

It'll hit so hard

It'll take your breath

The amount of love is the depth

The depth of which you grieve

But even still you have to believe

There is a God above

Who is watching and holding you with His love

You can't always feel

But that doesn't mean He's not real

1-19-17

"AT LAST"

Ahh, at last

Bringing up happy memories from the past

Four months have come and gone since I've been to Henpeck

Oh, but my friends act like I never left

I was greeted with the biggest hugs and smiles

Just to feel and see that made this spontaneous journey worth every single mile

Picking up like we never left off make this girl rather happy

Bittersweet and sappy

I sure do miss my friends here at Henpeck Market Village

Here's to more memories to be made

Hoping, over time, that they never fade

2-11-17

"HENPECK MARKET VILLAGE"

Henpeck Market Village, so much love is felt here

So much love, happiness and good cheer

Memories and friendships made to last long after you leave

Come as strangers, leave as friends is true, I do believe

If you're lucky like me

You might even become part of the Henpeck family

2-11-17

"HAPPY ANYWHERE?"

Happy here? Happy there?

I'm not happy anywhere

No more smiles dancing upon my face

I can't take any more heartbreak

They say no one dies from a broken heart

Maybe, but I know I'm falling apart

No more joy here to find

Is it hiding deep in the mind?

In a place I cannot reach

Maybe the way there is too hard to see

Maybe that's why my mind keeps it from me

All I know is, I'm not happy here or there

I'm not happy anywhere

2-17-17

"AT THE CROSS"

Here at the cross

Sitting, on my favorite rock

Gentle breeze blowing,

Brightly, in front of me, the sun is glowing

Soon to be setting behind the trees

Soon all that will be left are these precious memories

And the cross that's currently sitting behind me

Long after I leave,

People will continue to come and to see

To see the cross and all of the beauty

The beauty that surrounds

And will keep many people coming, from all around

2-17-17

"STRANGE"

It's strange how people, places and faces change

Especially the ones you wanted to stay the same

Dropped in to one of my favorite places

To find almost all new faces

A dear friend of mine still here for now

Though I don't know how

She doesn't seem like her usual happy self anymore

It hurts my heart to think she might have to walk out that door

She and some old friends are the reason I came

But now nothing's the same

I want things back to the way they were happy, bright, friendly and fun

Looks like those days are done

A piece of my heart gone forever

Thankful for the times we had together

Times where strangers became friends

Then when those friends became family to me

Those times were so special and happy

The times when my "family" helped my heart mend

Due to new owners, it all came to an end

This was a once in a lifetime place

All smiling faces have now gone away

4-29-17

"No Words"

Sitting outside, wind blowing

Music playing

Nothing to say, not today

Just sitting with a solemn look on my face

Hiding in the shadows of the fading sun

Trying not to feel that loss all over again

Gritting my teeth, fighting back tears

Hoping darkness doesn't bring back those suppressed fears

Hoping not to relive the panic from that day

Sitting here, no words to say

5-1-17

"THE MOMENT"

The moment you stopped caring

Was when I learned to stop sharing

Sharing my deepest thoughts and fears

And the tears that I built up over the years

The tears that hide the hurt, anger, frustration and pain

Are no longer there for your gain

You caught me in a time of grieving

You caught me when my heart stopped "beating"

You got what you wanted and now you're leaving

I loved you

And thought you did too

I guess I was wrong for believing

Believing without seeing

Seeing you for what you truly are

I'm sorry we even made it this far

Thanks for helping me lose trust again

Thanks for making me feel like you were my "friend"

Thanks for not being there for me in the end

5-15-17

"LONELY TRAVELER"

Lonely traveler, where are you headed?

I can tell you dread it

What's hurts you so bad?

What makes your heart so sad?

Why do you travel alone?

Why do you refuse to pick up the phone?

Why don't you say what you want to?

Why do you feel like this is what you have to do?

Why do you feel you have to travel alone?

Why do you feel like you have to have a turned off phone?

5-27-17

"LEAF IN THE WIND"

Things will be differently the same

Just as quickly as she came

She left, going around the bend

Like a fall leaf blowing in the wind

6-9-17

"THAT DAY"

Since the day my daddy died

All I've been able to do is cry

That day my world shattered

Leaving my heart bent, broken and tattered

Many losses I have had

But none compare to that of my dad

My dreams came to a halt

The moment his heart stopped

Carry on, people say,

Your dad wouldn't want you that way

But, people, understand I'm grieving the loss of my dad

A man who lived and loved

A man who is now up above

Why did he leave me here?

How do I get over all of this fear?

How do I live without my best friend?

How do I help my heart to mend?

How do I go on living?

How do I forgive the God who took him?

I don't want to be angry and bitter

I don't want to be a quitter

Closer to giving up with each passing day

I just don't understand why it's this way

6-19-17

"I DIED TOO"

A life cut short, gone too soon
And a shattered heart, left alone
From nightly I love you calls
To grief stricken as night around me falls
Tears filling the void in the night
Are the reason I still fight
To hear his voice again one day
I hope will be worth this terrible wait
I dread the days as morning draws near
Nothing's the same without him here
Stifled screams
Scary dreams
Surely he didn't want this for me
But it's him I can't see
Some days are better
Somedays it depends on the weather
The sun still comes up each morning
And leaves my heart mourning
The moon still hangs in the night sky
And I'm here wondering why
How does life go on without you here?
Why does the world still spin
And the leaves still blow in the wind?
Don't they know you're gone?
Unlike them, I can't seem to move on
I can't give up the person you were
I can't believe you left this earth
I know it wasn't your choice
But in a sense I've lost my voice
The day you left was the day I lost my life too

Just not in the same way as you
My shattered heart
Continues to tear me apart
The days are dimmer
And the nights longer
I died too
The day I lost you

6-24-17

"PEACE AGAIN"

Ahh, at last, some peace

Out here on the water in the open breeze

Sitting here listening

To the hum of the jet ski

Waves crashing on the rocks

Resting on the boat in the dock

Close your eyes

Much to your surprise

Peace again

Just God, me, the water, and the wind

7-9-17

"IT KEEPS GOING"

Time marches on
Even with you gone
Minutes flash into hours,
Hours into days.
Days in weeks,
And weeks into months,
Months fade into years
But my eyes are still full of tears

7-10-17

"LEAVE SOMETHING"

Even in you feel like a hot mess,

Take those pictures no one cares how you're dressed

Even if you can't sing, sing

Write something, anything

Leave something behind for those you love

Let them know you're thinking of them from up above

Give them those memories to hold onto

Until the next time they see you

7-10-17

"FINAL REQUEST"

I wish to express

My final request

Cry not for the life that is gone

For God and me it's another precious victory won

A life full of sadness and tears

A life full of anxiety and fears

Is now a life with light and hope

And smiles for miles

I'll have no more cares

I'll be waiting for you there

7-11-17

"WAITING THERE"

The life I had here was a life well spent

It was a life well lived with family and friends

A life of "get up and go's"

Now gone, like a vapor in the wind

A heart so loved

Now resting with the Father up above

One last wish remains

That you'll join me in Heaven someday

When your time comes, as mine did

I hope you hear Him say come my child, come in

Into the gates of pearls and the streets of gold

Living the stories you've always been told

You'll lay down thy staff and thy rod

When you enter the Kingdom of God

You'll see angels everywhere

You'll see me again, waiting for you there

7-11-17

"BEYOND FOREVER"

I love you,

I love you beyond the moon

Beyond the vast sea and skies

I love you higher than the rockets can fly

I love you more with each passing day

I love you more than I could ever say

I am truly blessed to call you mine

You always make my world shine

Your laughter is my favorite sound

It can turn any bad day around

Oh and your smile,

Makes everything worth while

I love you beyond forever and a day

I love your gentle ways

I love and accept all of you

And I know you feel this way too

7-25-17

"Here with you"

Being back here with you
Is one of my favorite things to do
Back where chaos and peace unite
Back to the spiritual light
Bells ringing from afar
Reminds us of where we are,
In the peaceful garden, hidden from the city
On a day like today, it's oh so pretty
The crows are cawing in the background
Do you hear all of those nature sounds?
Birds chirping in the trees
And the wind gently blowing the leaves
The green grass shines in the light
And the sun is shining bright

7-30-17

"It's me"

Hey, it's me

This time it's your grave I came to see

From life to love

And from the ground to up above

I know you surround me in your love

But I miss you today

I miss you always

Not a day goes by that I don't think of you

And wonder what you'd be up to

Playing jokes on me,

Traveling city to city

Wake up calls

I love you's as night falls

I miss your laugh so much it hurts

I miss the lessons learned

I miss the life we had

But mostly, I miss you dad

I miss the belly laughs

And the horses we'd try to catch

I miss our talks,

I miss our walks

Toward the setting sun

I miss you and all of our fun

I miss your big smile

It kept me going for many miles

(continued)

(continued)

But dad, missing you won't bring you back to me

So, I'm waiting patiently

Waiting to come see you in the sky

Waiting to gain my wings to fly

I feel you everywhere

But I'll keep waiting to see you there

8-12-17

"I'M HERE"

Hey dad, I'm here

Overcoming my fear

I came, dad

And I'm celebrating the life you had

Thank you for being the best

I am truly blessed

Blessed to have had you for the time that I did

Blessed to be surrounded in your spirit

Some peace surrounds me now

As I sit here, under the clouds

There's a gentle breeze blowing

And the grass is growing

I hear all the nature sounds

Now that I've turned my music down

I'm here, dad

Celebrating the life you had

8-12-17

"DON'T GIVE UP ON ME"

If you love me,

Don't give up on me

When you hear me screaming at night

Know that's me not willing to give up the fight

Nights are hard on me,

They bring anxiety

And the inability to sleep

They bring an overload of tears

And irrational fears

Don't give up on me

When the hard nights come,

Just pray I make it to the morning sun

9-5-17

"HOLDING ON TO HOPE"

I'm holding on to the hope
That you'll never let me go
I know you're always by my side
Even in the dark of the night
You provide peace
Even when I can't see
When I can't see
What the future holds
You're there with a ray of hope
You light the path for me
You help me to see
You let me know I'm gonna be alright
That there's hope in the darkest night
Thank you for not giving up on me
And for giving me the time I need
Thank you for the hope and peace
Most importantly,
Thank you for loving me

9-7-17

"WHAT DO I SHOW?"

What part of me do I show the world?

The part of me that is cold and surled?

The part I keep hidden

Because how I feel is forbidden?

The happy light-hearted side

With my arms open wide?

The lonely and sad

That reflects the day I've had?

The "I'm fine, and you?"

That society tells us to do?

Or do I show the raw and painful truth?

Do I keep showing the world I'm ok?

While I'm staring at my crying face

In the mirror?

Or do I learn to be dear

To those who are around

And hope they don't see the same thing I've found?

9-8-17

"BROKENNESS"

Hurting eyes, broken smile

And a heart that's been mending for a while

Have all been hiding

Behind this big fake smile

Brokenness has become a part of me

It's the part I don't let others see

It's the part that makes me who I am

After everything else has torn me down

9-8-17

"How do I move on?"

My heart has been ripped from my chest

Is this come cruel test?

Tears flood from my face

Will I ever find peace?

It feels like hell on earth without you

My heart is so confused

I know you're at peace

But I'm left here full of grief

I scream and cry for you still

It doesn't feel right to feel it to this intensity

Why is everything so extreme?

Why did you leave?

Why do the nights and thoughts of you still consume me?

I don't know how to live with you gone

Tell me, how do I move on?

9-17-17

"Shadow"

Oh, that shadow on the ground

It follows me all around

It has followed me through trials and fights

It has followed me through all of the perilous days and nights

It has been there on the good days and the bad

It's been through all the happy and sad

It's been there through it all

But my shadow still stands tall

9-9-17

AFTERWORD

As the author of this book, I feel it is important to share with you why it was written. This book came into fruition in both times of hope and deep despair. It addresses topics that we all face on our own personal journeys and reminds us that we are not alone. Depression, addiction, grief, loss, suffering and even anger, are just a few things I struggle with immensely, even to this day. This has not been an easy road to travel, but I have realized that my life is an assignment from God. Our journey of struggles and triumphs are part of our assigned growth processes. My message to you is that you're going to be ok. There is always *hope*. For a long time, I wondered whether or not I could allow myself to be vulnerable to you, my friend.

I decided I would bare my soul, because someone out there, maybe you, need to know that someone else is in a similar position or feels what you are feeling. In the depths of despair, it is hard not to give up, but please don't. Someone needs you. You are important, and you matter, more than you will ever know. Please keep fighting for those "good" or "better" moments.

The times of darkness are only temporary. Please know this. It took me a while to realize the truth and power of that statement. Glimmers and rays of light and hope have never failed to arise. We all experience times of darkness and times of light, but I could not live without having hope in God. Even when I was angry toward Him, He never left me. It took a long time to realize God is big enough to handle my anger, and He is also patient enough to wait for the anger to pass.

Remember there is always hope for you, even in your darkest hour, as there is for me. My deepest wish for you is that you will find comfort, peace, and solace in knowing you are never truly alone, for God is with you, just as He is with me.

Much love,
Brooksie D. Thompson

ABOUT THE AUTHOR

Combining her passions for writing and helping others, Brooke Thompson champions the well-being of those in need through her art. Shedding light on personal trauma, Brooke hopes to build bridges between those in pain and a healthy, alternative support system made up of words, lines, and stanzas. Having been writing for more than a decade, Brooke has published not one, or two, but three books of poetry that explore the spectrum of the human experience. From grief and loss to love, hope, and change, the breadth of emotion and scope of understanding that Brooke brings to her craft is a true testament to her passion for writing and her dedication to providing support, hope, and aid.

Not content to just write and share, Brooke is an advocate for mental health reform and uses her writing as a tool for raising awareness. Currently pursuing a degree in counseling, Brooke hopes to one day translate her background in advocacy to a job as a counselor. Her greatest hope is to use her dual careers, writing and mental health care, to reach others in their darkest hour.

A native of Texas, Brooke now hangs her hat in Nashville, TN, but her heart and the place she calls home will always be in her beautiful small hometown Waynesboro, TN.

Be sure to check out Brooke's website: brooksiedthompson.com
Blog: getalookintobrooke.blogspot.com

81

Made in the USA
Middletown, DE
09 March 2019